The

WELSH POTTERY

Lynne Bebb

1. Two South Wales Pottery plates, 170 mm in diameter, decorated with the stylised hand-painted 'Cockerel' design, said to have been the invention of Sarah Roberts, or Aunty Sal as she was known, one of the paintresses at the factory at the end of the nineteenth century. The design is found with a variety of sponge-decorated border patterns on dishes and plates, and more rarely on mugs, and is sometimes inscribed with dates as late as 1913. This design is never marked but thought to be exclusive to the South Wales Pottery.

Printed in Great Britain by CIT Printing
Services, Press Buildings, Merlins Bridge,
Haverfordwest, Pembrokeshire SA61 1XF.

British Library Cataloguing in Publication Data:
Bebb, Lynne. Welsh Pottery. - (The Shire Book)
1. Pottery, Welsh 2. Pottery, Welsh - History
I. Title 738'.09429
ISBN 0 7478 0339 0

Published in 1997 by Shire Publications Ltd,
Cromwell House, Church Street, Princes
Risborough, Buckinghamshire HP27 9AA, UK.
Copyright © 1997 by Lynne Bebb. First published
1997. ISBN 0 7478 0339 0.
Lynne Bebb is hereby identified as the author of
this work in accordance with Section 77 of the
Copyright, Designs and Patents Act 1988.

ACKNOWLEDGEMENTS
I wish to thank those local collectors who allowed me to photograph their pieces
and in particular Phil Jones and Clive Reed for sharing their knowledge of the
Ynysmeudwy pottery. All photographs are courtesy of Country Antiques (Wales),
Kidwelly, Carmarthenshire.

NOTE
Place-names in Wales frequently have alternative Welsh and English spellings. The
versions current at the periods under discussion have been used in the text, as
these are often included in marks.

COVER PHOTOGRAPH
*A South Wales Pottery plate, 250 mm in diameter, hand-painted by Samuel Shufflebotham, signed
on the front with his initials 'S.W.S.', and marked on the back 'Llanelly' in green stencilled letters.
The design depicts a woman in Welsh costume with the word 'Wales' and was made between
1908 and 1915.*

CONTENTS

EARLY POTTERY IN WALES

Archaeological records confirm the use of pottery throughout Wales from prehistoric times, but it is less clear whether it was of local origin. It is generally thought that from the breakdown of the Roman Empire until the Norman invasion vessels of metal, wood, leather and horn were more favoured alternatives to pottery, but following the Norman Conquest a flourishing trade in pottery developed, importing wares from England and overseas. However, evidence obtained during excavations suggests that some at least of the pottery was made close to where it was found.

Microscopic examination of clay reveals characteristics which tie it to an area of origin. By examining particles in the fabric of medieval sherds from South Wales, it is possible to identify three distinct types of clay and archaeologists have recognised three areas of production: south-west Wales, north Gwent and the Vale of Glamorgan.

Further evidence is provided by the discovery of kiln sites or kiln furniture, and by sherds unearthed in such quantities as to suggest a site of manufacture. Kiln sites discovered at Newport, Pembrokeshire, and Ewloe, Flintshire, confirm ceramic production in the middle ages. Finds as far apart as Swansea, Monmouth, Ewenny in Glamorgan and Buckley in Flintshire have established the widespread presence of working kilns in the post-medieval period.

Place-names suggesting the existence of a pottery are found throughout Wales. There is, for example, a Pwllcrochan (Crock Pool) in Pembrokeshire. In 1427 a site called Potterisland, in the Ewenny area, was leased from Sir John Stradling, and downstream from Ogmore Castle there was another Pwll Crochan.

Documents such as parish records, tithe maps and estate papers have revealed sources of potting clay, identified land used in connection with the manufacture of pottery and named men and women in pottery-related occupations. A thirteenth-century subsidy roll from Ewloe names a John le Potter and a Robert le Potter, and in 1756 David Arthur, potter, is recorded in Swansea Corporation rent rolls as digging clay on the Burroughs.

Pottery distributed over a wide area is difficult to attribute to a particular centre of production. In the absence of other evidence to verify a local origin, trade records can establish the kinds of pottery imported or show that pottery was traded from a particular place, which might point to the existence of an indigenous ceramics industry. Coastal trade was well developed in Wales, and port records show that in the seventeenth and eighteenth centuries pottery was imported into South Wales from Devon and Bristol.

Despite the influx of imports, evidence points to a widespread and economically important manufacture of coarse wares. The earliest pottery was hand-built and fired on a bonfire or in a pitclamp. By the middle ages pots might be turned on crude wheels and fired in primitive kilns with single flues. Kilns were built close to sources of potting clay, water, fuel and the materials used for tempering the clay and glazing the finished pots. These were made to supply local needs for vessels for the storage and preparation of food.

Pots were functional and bore little or no decoration apart from incised marks, slip-trailed designs and simple applied mouldings. Lead glazes were sometimes used but were confined to the exterior. Forms included jugs, cooking pots, mugs with many handles (tygs), bowls, jars and pitchers. Shapes were dictated by the specific purposes they were meant to fulfil, by the possibilities of the medium and by the limitations of the technology. Because they were produced to supply local needs they remained relatively free from outside influences, but at this stage there was little that was characteristically Welsh.

At the beginning of the seventeenth century large quantities of pottery from North Devon were imported into South Wales specifically for use in the trade of Welsh butter, which was exported as far as the colonies. The pots were used as packaging, ideal for keeping the butter in good condition, but also acting as units of measurement. Nevertheless, as archaeological evidence from the period accumulates, it is clear that a significant indigenous industry also flourished throughout Wales. Kilns were still located close to necessary resources but were more sophisticated. Pots were produced on blacksmith-made wheels, or sometimes by simple press moulds. Potteries were essentially small-scale and labour-intensive, with little specialisation. They produced wares which satisfied local demands for ceramics for a wide range of domestic and farm uses.

2. Miscellaneous collection of thrown coarseware fulfilling a variety of functions in the home and dairy and made by small-scale pottery producers such as those at Buckley and Ewenny.

5

SMALL-SCALE PRODUCTION

The two best-documented centres for pottery production in Wales in the late seventeenth and early eighteenth centuries are Buckley in Flintshire and Ewenny in Glamorgan. Although the generic terms 'Buckley' and 'Ewenny' are given to pottery from the two areas, they apply to concentrations of independent working kilns, which were typical of the post-medieval period. Each kiln was built and operated by members of the same family, and every worker, including women and children, would have been capable, if required, of assisting in every stage of production.

First the clay was dug, carted to the pottery and left to mature. It was then refined, with organic impurities and large particles being removed. After this, tempering (coarse sand, gravel or ground flint) was added where necessary and the clay was made up into balls of the right size for each job. It was thrown on a wheel, either operated by a treadle or hand-turned by a boy or potter's assistant, and drawn up into the required shape. At this stage the pots were left to become leather-hard, after which handles were added and the pots were decorated, using various techniques, and then glazed.

The glazed pots were left to dry, and when sufficient pots had accumulated, after about four weeks, they were carefully stacked into the kiln. Glazed surfaces were separated by small ceramic props or stilts, and delicate pieces were packed inside large fireclay vessels or saggars, for protection during firing. Once the pots were stacked, the kiln was closed and the temperature was slowly raised. The right temperature was maintained by opening and closing flues controlling air intake. The correct firing procedure required considerable skill.

Finally the wares had to be marketed, either sold on site or carried by cart, packhorse or boat to markets further afield.

3. Buckley dish of red earthenware, 318 mm long, 254 mm wide, glazed inside with slip-trailed decoration.

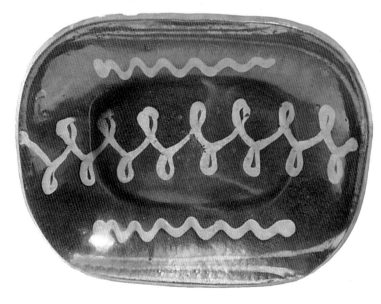

4. Buckley round platter of red earthenware, 343 mm in diameter, with piecrust edge and dragged slip decoration.

Each pottery would have kept a horse or two, both for transport and to drive the mill wheels which ground tempering and the ingredients for glazes. Whenever possible pots were sent by water, a safer and cheaper means of transport for fragile commodities. Easy access to the coast or inland waterways was a considerable advantage for a pottery.

BUCKLEY

Although pottery production in Buckley began in the medieval period, the first known kiln dates from the early seventeenth century. The kilns were grouped on Buckley Mountain, close to almost inexhaustible supplies of clay and coal, and to sources of lead, used in the production of glazes. They produced domestic wares, either wheel-thrown or formed on simple convex press moulds. The fabric when fired ranged in colour from buff through to pink, red and purple. The forms were simple in shape but well thrown and eminently suited to their purpose: pans, bowls, platters, tankards, storage jars, dripping pans, etc.

5. Large Buckley jug of red earthenware, 260 mm high, with the typical distinctive black glaze.

7

Above left. 6.
Buckley flower pot on stand, 230 mm in diameter, 305 mm high, made from red earthenware covered with white slip into which are inscribed 'June 1907' and '1907'.

Above right. 7.
Buckley three-tiered money box, 292 mm high, decorated with birds (damaged) and inscribed 'Jane Molineux 9 Priory Hill Everton Liverpool'; made towards the end of the nineteenth century.

For a brief period early pots were decorated with elaborate sgraffito designs which were scratched into a layer of light-coloured slip (a mixture of clay and water, applied in a liquid state). These were based upon traditional images of fabulous beasts. Other techniques of slip decoration were more common. Sometimes slips of several colours were applied to dishes or plates and, while still wet, swirled about to create spiral patterns (joggling), or tools were dragged across the surface to create lattice designs. Everyday wares were given bands of light-coloured slip or had a sharp tool or the potter's knuckle held against them during throwing to raise decorative rills. Occasionally different-coloured clays were combined to produce the marbled effect of agate. Dedications, dates or the names of people and places were frequently inscribed, and later wares often bore references to food such as beef, pork, lamb or pie. Buckley is best-known for its large platters with piecrust edges, to which trails of light-coloured slip were applied in free-flowing designs, and for wares with a high-gloss dark brown or black glaze.

Before industrialisation the market for Buckley ware was substantial, supplying as it did the needs of a rural economy. Buckley pottery was traded throughout Wales and to Ireland, taking full advantage of the easy access to coastal shipping along the numerous rivers and, later, canals. It is, however, rarely marked and few, if any, shapes or decorative techniques were exclusive to the area. There were many similarities to pottery produced in Staffordshire. Identification can often be confirmed by good provenance and strong probability or when sherds from similar vessels have been found at a Buckley kiln site.

EWENNY

Ewenny is situated in the Vale of Glamorgan south of Bridgend, where there are deep deposits of good potting clay, with coal supplies close by. The clay needs no tempering, although limestone impurities have to be carefully removed to prevent excessive pitting during firing. Production probably began in the middle ages, but there is no supporting archaeological evidence. Documentary evidence from the eighteenth century identifies twelve named potters and five working kilns. Fifteen small family-run kilns are thought to have existed, scattered about the vicinity, but with no more than seven in operation at any one time.

As industrialisation gathered pace in the early nineteenth century and the population in the area grew, production expanded to meet the increased demand for household vessels. At the same time the decline of the North Devon potteries reduced the competition, giving further encouragement to the proliferation of small concerns run on traditional lines.

Large quantities of useful red earthenware pots were produced, including milk pans, colanders, porringers, jars, jugs, wash bowls and chamber pots. These were glazed and decorated with simple slip-trailed designs or banding. More decorative items were also made with elaborate sgraffito designs, such as jugs and shaving mugs. Sometimes plants were pressed into the still wet pots and covered with slip. The plants burnt away in the kiln, leaving their imprint behind. Decorative money boxes with modelled birds and puzzle jugs with sgraffito designs were also made, many bearing dates and inscriptions. Ewenny pots are frequently marked and dated.

The most spectacular of Ewenny products were the wassail bowls or *ffiol dolenog*, with eighteen handles. These were decorated with leaves, hop plants and compass-

Top. 8. Ewenny shaving mug of red earthenware, 178 mm high, 120 mm in diameter, glazed inside and decorated with sgraffito designs in slip, inscribed 'Robert Jones owner made at Eweney July 2 1842'.

Above. 9. Ewenny model elephant and baby, 120 mm high, 152 mm long, 90 mm wide, in red earthenware, glazed over slip, with the Welsh inscriptions 'Wyf yn gryf Cawrfil' ('I am a strong elephant') and 'Baban wyf' ('I am a baby') and inscribed on the bottom 'Jones Bridgend Ewenny'.

9

10. Wassail bowl standing 395 mm high and inscribed: 'Mary Hopkins married the 30th Day of April 1837, Gift of William Thomas, Claypits'. William Thomas was the owner of the Claypits pottery at Ewenny at this time. A seated figure is missing from the lid, which is profusely decorated with birds and moulded motifs. In the early nineteenth century such bowls were used in the traditional Vale of Glamorgan New Year wassailing celebrations. Ribbons were attached to the handles, and the bowls, filled with ale, were taken in procession from house to house.

drawn designs scratched into light-coloured slip. There were modelled and moulded decorations on the conical domed lid, including birds and animals and sometimes a figure seated at a table with food and drink. They were often given as gifts, with the name of the owner and sometimes the donor inscribed. Occasionally the maker is named.

Towards the end of the nineteenth century tastes had changed, and cheap white earthenwares and enamelled metal goods supplied many traditional needs, displacing the products of country potteries, which consequently faltered. Some of the Buckley potteries switched to the manufacture of bricks and tiles. However, influenced by the Arts and Crafts movement, most of the kilns in both Buckley and Ewenny halted the decline by turning out novelty wares, with inscriptions, and experimental shapes and glazes. Ewenny inscriptions were often in Welsh. The market for these decorative wares supported pottery production in both areas well into the twentieth century; indeed two potteries were still in operation at Ewenny in 1997.

Far left. 11. Ewenny press-moulded cat, 368 mm high, made from red earthenware covered with light slip and glazed. Inscribed on the bottom '1917 Ewenny Pottery' with the number 198.

Left. 12. Beautifully crafted tall jug, 470 mm high, hand-thrown in buff-coloured clay, with an attractive decorative green glaze. Marked 'Ewenny Pottery', the jug was probably made in the early twentieth century and is a fine example of the skill of the Ewenny potters.

NINETEENTH-CENTURY INDUSTRIAL PRODUCTION

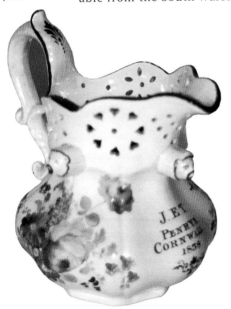

13. Cambrian puzzle jug, 190 mm high, decorated with hand-painted flowers and the dedication 'J.E.T. PENRYN CORNWALL 1835'. This pouch shape is typical of Cambrian jugs of the period 1830-51. In addition to this delicate hand-painting, they are found decorated with transfers, applied mouldings, coloured glazes and in the 'Gaudy Welsh' manner. Jugs often bore dedications, and from 1836 to 1847 they were sometimes made in earthenware fired at a higher temperature and marked 'Cymro Stone China' in a raised pad.

In 1791 the English East India Company, which monopolised the trade in oriental porcelain, stopped importing on a large scale and thus a huge gap was created in the market for decorated wares. The company had accused London china dealers of cheating by conspiring to hold down the price of the porcelain at the auctions through which it was distributed. Meanwhile, technical innovations pioneered by Josiah Wedgwood since the 1760s had made possible the production of cheap white earthenware, which potteries throughout Britain and elsewhere began to imitate. Investment in potteries increased as industrialisation took hold. New factories sprang up, based for the first time on production lines. The production process was divided into separate stages, each assigned to teams organised around key skilled workers. Pottery work was still a family affair, and teams might include several members of the same family, male and female. Such specialisation meant that pottery workers, though highly skilled in one aspect of production, no longer had any responsibility or even sometimes any knowledge of other stages of manufacture.

THE CAMBRIAN POTTERY

All the requirements for the industrial production of ceramics were to be found in the Swansea Valley in west Glamorgan. There was a port through which to import raw materials and export finished wares. Fuel was readily available from the South Wales coalfields. Well-established trade routes and a developing home market ensured demand, and there were plenty of local entrepreneurs ready to expand and diversify their businesses.

One such man was William Coles, who in 1764 negotiated with Swansea Corporation to demolish the old copper works and erect a pottery in its place. Production began around 1768 and was confined at first to coarse wares made from local clay. These were red, yellow or buff in colour and lead-glazed. Early success and the example set by the Wedgwood factory in Staffordshire prompted new developments and superior white ball clay began to be imported from Devon for the

11

14. *Cambrian jug, 255 mm high, decorated with an oriental transfer design in black, probably engraved by Thomas Rothwell; made between 1797 and 1800.*

15. *Cambrian puzzle jug, 203 mm high, decorated with a blue transfer oriental flower design, 1800-16. Puzzle jugs, which could be used only by covering up all the holes but one, were also made at the Glamorgan Pottery.*

production of fine-quality white earthenware and creamware. China clay was added later at the Cambrian Pottery, but at first only in very small quantities. Whiteness was achieved by the use of calcinated ground flint and the addition of cobalt oxide to both the clay body and the glazes, giving early Cambrian pottery a characteristic bluish tinge.

In 1778 William Coles died, leaving the pottery to his three sons. Shortly afterwards George Haynes took over the day-to-day running of the factory. Like the Coles family, he was not a potter but an energetic and capable manager. Haynes extensively reorganised the production and substantially improved the quality. At first the pottery employed local labour, but Haynes encouraged skilled potters from Staffordshire to move to the area and they brought knowledge, expertise and the latest techniques in what at that time was a growing industry. Fine earthenware and creamware decorated with both transfers and hand painting were made during this period.

At first the pottery traded under the name of Coles & Haynes, and it is possible that Haynes became a partner. The better-known title 'Cambrian' was adopted shortly afterwards and retained until the works finally ceased trading.

All the potteries of South Wales changed hands throughout their history. The wares which characterised various periods of ownership often carried marks incorporating the names or initials of the factory's owners. It is important for the purposes of identification and dating to understand something of the sequence of ownership. At the Cambrian Pottery Haynes was left in sole charge in 1799 when John Coles died, but in 1801 the lease was bought by William Dillwyn, a Quaker businessman, who handed it to his son, Lewis Weston Dillwyn.

Top right. *16. Cambrian plate, 240 mm in diameter, with a hand-painted scene in sepia, and grape and vine border decoration and gilding, possibly the work of Thomas Pardoe, and inscribed on the bottom 'Table Cove Isle of Wight'; made between 1797 and 1810.*

Centre right. *17. Cambrian plate, 200 mm by 140 mm, decorated in blue with the 'Monopteros' pattern, one of the few new transfer designs to emerge during the Bevington period, 1817-24.*

Bottom right. *18. Cambrian plate, 230 mm in diameter, decorated with a black transfer ship design, impressed 'DILLWYN' over 'SWANSEA' in a horseshoe shape, with a G transfer mark in blue, made between 1831 and 1851; also found in blue and occasionally with initials. Ship designs were popular and several were produced by both the Cambrian and Glamorgan factories.*

Haynes was retained as manager but left in 1810. Dillwyn then took Timothy Bevington and his son into partnership, and the manufacture of Swansea porcelain began. Dillwyn briefly relinquished his interest in the works in favour of the Bevingtons, but they proved unable to manufacture profitably.

After 1824, when Dillwyn resumed sole ownership, earthenware production continued at the Cambrian factory, even though porcelain was abandoned. Fine-quality transfer decoration and stylised hand painting characterised this period and continued to do so when Lewis Llewelyn Dillwyn took over from his father. He and his wife developed black Etruscan Ware, an attempt to produce a quality product at a price that ordinary people could afford. The venture failed, and Dillwyn sold the pottery to Evans and Glasson. D. J. Evans went into partnership with his son following Glasson's death shortly afterwards. Evans was unable to maintain the quality of the product, and the business finally closed in 1870.

THE GLAMORGAN POTTERY
Although it was the first factory to open in Swansea, the Cambrian did not corner the market. The

principal challenge was mounted by the Glamorgan Pottery, which began operating in 1813 on a site next to the Cambrian. It was owned by the partnership of Baker, Bevans and Irwin and managed by George Haynes's son-in-law William Baker. The new pottery began producing good-quality earthenware, rivalling the Cambrian, until 1838, when it was bought up by Dillwyn and closed down to eliminate the competition. The Glamorgan shapes were similar to those of the Cambrian, but distinguishable from them, and were decorated with transfers and simple hand painting.

OTHER SWANSEA FACTORIES
Also in Swansea, the Dyvatty Street or Pleasant Vale Pottery, founded in the 1840s, produced domestic earthenware but was principally known for making pitchers for collecting water from street pumps. It closed in 1892. White earthenware was also made at the Calland Pottery at Landore, which operated briefly from 1852 to 1856.

19. Glamorgan moulded plate 215 mm in diameter, glazed with an iridescent green glaze; also found occasionally with a dark blue glaze.

YNYSMEUDWY
There was also a productive pottery at Ynysmeudwy, in the Tawe valley on the banks of the Swansea Canal. It was founded in 1845 by two Cornish brothers, Michael and William Williams, and began making coarse earthenware and bricks. The village of Ynysmeudwy grew up around the pottery, and the Williams

20. Ynysmeudwy moulded meat plate, 455 mm by 360 mm, decorated with the transfer design 'Rio' in brown, a pattern thought to be exclusive to Ynysmeudwy. The pattern is also found in blue or flow-blue on a range of items including tea bowls, tureens and coffee pots.

14

Above. *21. South Wales Pottery chestnut basket, 230 mm by 170 mm, marked 'Llanelly Art Pottery'. Usually found with a similar pierced stand, decorated with transfers or hand-painted flowers, the design is sometimes attributed to Frederick Henshall, a member of a large potting family working at the factory in the late nineteenth century. Examples of similar size and shape have, however, been attributed to the Glamorgan Pottery.*

Right. *22. Three-piece South Wales Pottery shaving mug, 240 mm high, with transfer decoration in pink of biblical scenes, 'Moses striking the rock' on one side and 'The Good Shepherd' on the other, with 'Shell' border and the inscription in black cursive writing, 'A present for Captain Joseph Edmunds from Llanelly 1886'. Such inscriptions commemorating births, marriages, coming of age and so on were extremely popular and can be found on a wide range of pieces from small mugs to bread plates and ink pots as well as hand-painted wares.*

brothers built cottages for the mainly local workforce. White earthenware production started in 1849 and continued through changes of ownership until final closure in 1877. Wares of good quality were produced throughout its history, although only the earlier pieces were marked, and a wide range of shapes was decorated with transfers, lustre, slip decoration and hand painting.

SOUTH WALES POTTERY

In 1840 a new pottery was established at Llanelly in Carmarthenshire, 10 miles (16 km) west of Swansea, by William Chambers, a leading figure in the town. Like Swansea, Llanelly was well placed for the production of ceramics. The factory

23. South Wales Pottery plate, 250 mm in diameter, with decoration depicting Mari Jones, the devout Welsh girl who in the eighteenth century diligently saved and when she had enough money walked many miles to purchase a Bible. Hand-painted probably by Samuel Shufflebotham about 1910, stencil-marked 'LLANELLY' in green.

was managed by William Bryant, formerly employed at both the Cambrian and Glamorgan potteries. He signed up workers from Staffordshire as well as some of the redundant Glamorgan workforce. The demise of the Glamorgan factory and the subsequent movement of workers allowed the new undertaking to produce transfer-decorated wares to fill the gap left in the market by Glamorgan, although hand-painted pieces were also produced.

Known as the South Wales Pottery, the factory at Llanelly went through many changes of ownership, but throughout its history transfer-decorated pottery continued to be made for the home market and for export. At one time over half the factory's production was exported. The production of transfer-decorated ware was particularly strong from 1858 to 1869 under the ownership of William Holland. When the Cambrian Pottery closed in 1870, Holland bought up the copper plates which Dillwyn had retained from the Glamorgan works, and in 1870 he also bought up the Ynysmeudwy works. He was unable to exploit his advantage fully, and in 1875 the Llanelly factory closed for a short time. When it reopened in 1877 under the partnership of Guest and Dewsberry, the ceramics industry was being heavily influenced by the Arts and Crafts movement, and at Llanelly the emphasis was now placed on brightly coloured hand-painted wares.

By this time the growth of the railways had taken away the advantage that coastal access had given to South Wales. Staffordshire led the field once more. Though the factory at Llanelly outlasted its rivals, lack of investment brought about its gradual decline. In 1921, unable to withstand shrinking markets, the pottery closed and so the industrial production of ceramics in South Wales ended.

Above left. *24. Glamorgan cow creamer, 170 mm long, made around 1830. It is decorated with a black fishing scene from the Rural series and marked on the base 'Opaque China' over 'B. B. & I.' in a scroll with a transferrer's mark and an impressed '11'. The milk is put into a hole in the top, covered by the small lid, and poured out through the mouth using the tail as a handle. Transfer-decorated Glamorgan cows are usually marked, and a dark brown glaze and all-over purple lustre are also found.*

Above right. *25. Cambrian cow creamer, 180 mm long, on a green base, decorated with pink lustre flower heads and made around 1830. Cambrian cows are of stockier build than Glamorgan cows, with a more pronounced breast bone, and are usually decorated with crude pink lustre or brown flowers, although transfer decoration is also found. They are seldom marked, but an impressed 'D' was sometimes used. The South Wales Pottery also made cow creamers using a mould which appears to have been taken directly from a cow from one of the Swansea factories.*

SHAPES, PATTERNS AND MARKS

Early shapes produced at Swansea were basic, made of salt-glazed earthenware and decorated using a technique known as scratch blue, whereby a flower or a name and date were scratched into the surface, and blue cobalt was rubbed in. By the end of the eighteenth century the use of moulds became more widespread and shapes, no longer dictated by the technique of throwing, became more elaborate. When George Haynes took over at the Cambrian Pottery, the influence of Josiah Wedgwood, whom he greatly admired, became apparent in neo-classical shapes and designs. During this period the modeller George Bentley worked at the factory. Under his influence figures of Antony and Cleopatra, cupids, Egyptian candle holders and Roman lamps were produced, along with elaborate vases of cane-ware (a kind of stoneware) and game-pie dishes in buff-coloured clay.

As the population grew and new markets for cheap white wares developed, attention turned away from modelling of this kind. The Swansea factories concentrated on producing tea, dinner and supper services, toilet wares and all kinds of decorative jugs, plates, vases, bowls and ornaments. Plates with moulded feather edges, small moulded plates known locally as cockle plates and children's plates with moulded

17

Left. *26. Cambrian dish, 210 mm by 205 mm, decorated by Thomas Pardoe, after Curtis, with 'Round-leaved cyclamen' painted in green on the back and impressed 'SWANSEA'; typical of pieces made between 1802 and 1810.*

Below left. *27. A pierced wicker-bordered Glamorgan plate, 190 mm in diameter, decorated with the 'Ladies of Llangollen' transfer design, impressed 'BAKER BEVANS AND IRWIN' in a horseshoe over the Prince of Wales's feathers and 'SWANSEA'. The design was also used by the Cambrian factory although it is not clear where it originated. The design depicts the two celebrated Irish women who eloped to Wales in 1776 and settled at Plas Newydd, Llangollen, Denbighshire.*

Below right. *28. Cambrian plate, 190 mm in diameter, decorated by Thomas Pardoe, after Curtis, with 'Purple groundsel' painted on the back, impressed 'SWANSEA', made between 1802 and 1810. Hand-coloured botanical transfers, also after Curtis, were made between 1812 and 1817 but are distinguishable by a black outline.*

rims were made at most of the factories. Both Cambrian and Glamorgan made plates with pierced edges and cow creamers. Shapes followed contemporary trends, and silverware designs were much copied. A strong rococo influence was apparent in elaborate shapes and mouldings, but as the Arts and Crafts movement gathered momentum shapes tended to simplify, complementing the lively hand painting popular at the end of the nineteenth century. A proportion of the shapes can safely be associated with particular factories.

All the factories produced both underglaze and overglaze hand painting, the earliest designs demonstrating a strong oriental influence. Thomas Pardoe, the best-known of the Swansea pottery painters, worked at the Cambrian Pottery from 1795 to 1809. His repertoire included stylised flowers, land-

Left. 29. *A pierced wicker-bordered Cambrian plate 200 mm in diameter, decorated with a stylised tiger in pink lustre, made after 1824. Other subjects, including herons and cottages, are also found in pink lustre, and hand-painted flowers, transfers and canary lustre were used on such pieces, which are sometimes known as ribbon plates from the practice of threading ribbons through the perforations in order to hang them.*

Below. 30. *South Wales Pottery plate, 170 mm in diameter, with decoration depicting a Dutch girl, one of a series of Dutch subjects painted by Samuel Shufflebotham and marked with a hand-painted 'Llanelly', made around 1910.*

scapes, ornithological studies and insignia, and he was also a talented gilder. Under the influence of the botanist William Weston Young, a friend of Dillwyn who also painted a small amount of pottery, Pardoe produced a series of more accurate botanical studies copied from *Curtis Botanical Magazine*.

The best-known painter at the Glamorgan Pottery was William Pollard, who was born in Swansea in 1803 and trained at the Cambrian factory. He specialised in painting flowers and fruit.

The later period of hand painting at the South Wales Pottery is dominated by Samuel Shufflebotham, who came from Bristol in 1908. He painted flowers, fruit, rural scenes, cock and hen designs and figures and was heavily influenced by designs from Wemyss in Scotland.

But the history of pottery in South Wales can too easily be told by concentrating on the men who ran the factories and the well-known artists who worked there. The industry also relied heavily upon the skill and expertise of its workforce, many of whom were women. Women were responsible for significant quantities of all the hand-painted and sponge-decorated wares produced. Their considerable skill in applying colour with single brush strokes was instrumental in developing some of the most popular designs, including stylised flower painting and the Llanelly 'Persian Rose' and 'Cockerel' patterns. Some factories developed distinctive ranges of colours. The Glamorgan palette was bright with vibrant greens,

19

Above left. *31. Octagonal jug, 130 mm high, hand-painted with flowers, and impressed 'DILLWYN' over 'SWANSEA' in a horseshoe; made between 1830 and 1850.*

Above right. *32. Cambrian plate, 280 mm in diameter, hand-painted with a stylised flower spray demonstrating the freer, more expressive style of the period and marked with an impressed 'DILLWYN' over 'SWANSEA' in a horseshoe; made between 1824 and 1850.*

Below left. *33. Cambrian hand-painted plate, 240 mm in diameter, made between 1824 and 1850. Most of the South Wales factories produced similar hand-painted designs of stylised flowers.*

Below right. *34. Cambrian sponge-decorated plate, 240 mm in diameter, and impressed 'DILLWYN' over 'SWANSEA' in a horseshoe; made between 1824 and 1850. Large quantities of spongeware items of all kinds, particularly bowls, were made in South Wales both for the home market and for export, but they are very rarely marked.*

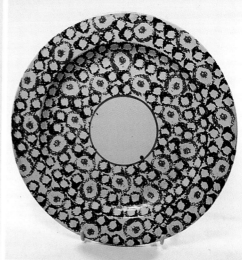

35. Three extremely rare hand-painted South Wales Pottery plates, from a group of five, each 248 mm in diameter but with a slightly different design. The style of painting is similar to work produced at the Cambrian and Glamorgan potteries and is possibly the work of one of the paintresses who came to the factory when the Glamorgan factory closed. The middle plate is marked 'SOUTH WALES POTTERY' in a horseshoe shape above the number 6. There are also painter's marks on each of the plates. The impressed mark belongs to the early Chambers period, 1840-55, after which impressed marks were no longer used at the factory.

36. South Wales Pottery pickle dish, 222 mm by 127 mm, hand-painted with the later 'Persian Rose' design. This bold stylised painting is typical of the later period and was used on a variety of shapes. The dish is unmarked but identical in size and shape to other examples.

37. South Wales Pottery platter, 290 mm by 230 mm, and a pickle dish, 222 mm by 127 mm. Both are decorated with a hand-painted design of 'Black Cherries', in a style normally attributed to Shufflebotham. The platter is marked 'Llanelly' in green on the back.

Left. *38. Cambrian dish, 140 mm in diameter, decorated with a transfer design in blue depicting an elephant with a howdah, probably the work of Thomas Rothwell, made between 1790 and 1800.*

Below. *39. Ynysmeudwy meat plate, 400 mm by 315 mm, decorated with the 'Oriental Birds' transfer pattern in blue, impressed 'YMP' and '14' with a transfer cartouche 'M.V. & Co.', which stands for a Staffordshire china retailer, Mellor, Venerables & Company. Pottery from South Wales is often found bearing such retailers' marks. This pattern was also applied to other items and a tureen similarly marked is known with a brown hand-coloured transfer. This pattern, amongst others, was also used at the South Wales Pottery after Ynysmeudwy was first taken over and then closed by W. T. Holland.*

oranges and rusts, as well as reds, yellows, blues and pinks. The Llanelly palette included black, red, green, cobalt blue and a muted yellow and, although a wider range was used, particularly in the later hand painting, it was always more restrained.

The South Wales potteries produced prodigious quantities of transfer-decorated wares. The technique of underglaze transfer decoration had been developed in the eighteenth century. Designs from engraved copper plates, inked with an oily cobalt blue mixture, were printed on to tissue paper. The wet printed paper was cut to fit the wares and pressed on. The paper was removed and the wares were glazed and fired.

40. Cambrian plate, 220 mm in diameter, one of a series of black transfer portraits with hand-painted borders in red and green, inscribed 'JAMES TEAR, PRESTON' and in script below the face 'The indefatigable Advocate of Total Abstinence from all intoxicating liquers'. It is impressed 'Dillwyn & Co' in a curve enclosing the number 7, made between 1831 and 1850. Other subjects include the Reverend John Fletcher, John Wesley and Prince Albert.

The earliest prints were inspired by oriental subjects, particularly the willow pattern, which was produced by every factory. Gradually new patterns were added, including flower designs and topographical subjects, which were printed on to every conceivable shape including cow creamers. Many designs were common to potteries all over Britain, but engravers such as Thomas Rothwell at the Cambrian and Herbert Toft and Robert Kent at the South Wales Pottery developed some which were unique, for example 'The Ladies of Llangollen' (see page 18), 'Women with Baskets', 'Vine Leaf and Flowers', 'The Haymaker', 'Llanelly Bouquet' and 'Flora'. The majority of transfer decoration is blue, but patterns were also printed in purple, black, green, pink and brown. Occasionally transfers of two colours were used on the same piece and some transfers were commonly augmented with hand colouring, for example 'Amherst Japan' and 'Whampoa'. Commemorative subjects and ship designs were also popular. Hand-painted dedications, names and dates were frequently added to both transfer-decorated and hand-painted wares.

Pink and copper lustre were used in hand-painted designs and some all-over copper lustreware was made, although, as such wares are rarely marked, the amount is a matter of dispute. Sherds dug up on the site of the Ynysmeudwy factory suggest that at least some of the copper lustre jugs found in Wales could have been produced there.

Most factories produced slip-decorated wares, including mocha and banding, for pubs and breweries. Jugs and mugs of standard capacities were marked with an embossed imperial mark or the local assay number but seldom bear a factory mark. Numerous sherds of cut slipware have also been unearthed at Ynysmeudwy.

Many of the ceramics at this time were marked on the base, with an impressed mark, a painted mark, a transfer or an

41. Cambrian jug, 140 mm high, decorated with a hand-coloured red transfer design showing Napoleon shackled in a field, surrounded by figures expressing anti-Napoleon sentiments. 'BONAPARTE DETHRONED April 1st 1814' is inscribed round the rim. This design is also found uncoloured on a yellow-ware jug of the same size and shape. Items of various kinds commemorating historic events were made by all the Swansea factories and were very popular.

42. South Wales Pottery jug, 150 mm high, which has been hand-coloured and marked on the bottom rim with an impressed 'SWP'.

43. Cambrian meat dish, 450 mm by 342 mm, and plate, 250 mm in diameter, decorated with 'Swansea Willow Pattern' transfer design, which is not a true willow pattern as it has minor additions and lacks the willow tree and the birds. Both pieces have the distinctive border which incorporates stylised moths and is thought to be exclusive to the Cambrian Pottery. The smaller plate has eight equidistant notches on the rim, a recognisable feature of the period, and the meat dish has an incised '18', which refers to size. Whole services were decorated in this manner, occasionally in brown, but mostly in a fine lustrous blue, sometimes with a brown rim. Made between 1797 and 1817.

inscription. Occasionally marks can be found incorporated into the decoration. Numerous numbers, letters and symbols were impressed or painted. These sometimes refer to shapes and sizes but they can also be marks made by potters, painters or transferrers as part of the piecework system.

Early creamware made at the Cambrian Pottery was marked 'SWANSEA' or 'CAMBRIAN' and some of Pardoe's work is signed. From 1802 'DILLWYN & Co' is found, sometimes incorporating 'SWANSEA' impressed in a circle or horseshoe. Between 1811 and 1817 'T & J BEVINGTON' was included, but from 1817 this appears alone. After 1824 pieces are impressed in a horseshoe 'DILLWYN', 'DILLWYN SWANSEA' or 'DILLWYN & Co'. Transfer cartouches bear the pattern name and sometimes the owners' names. After 1850 marks include 'EVANS & GLASSON', 'DAVID EVANS' and 'D. J. EVANS & Co'.

Impressed 'SWANSEA', 1790-1811.

Impressed 'DILLWYN & Co', 1802-17.

Impressed 'DILLWYN CAMBRIAN POTTERY SWANSEA', 1810-11.

Impressed 'DILLWYN & Co SWANSEA', 1811-30.

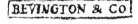

Impressed 'BEVINGTON & Co', 1817-24.

Transfer 'DILLWYN & Co SWANSEA', 1811-17.

Impressed 'SWANSEA POTTERY BEVINGTON & Co', 1817-24.

Transfer 'SWISS VILLA', 1824-36.

Transfer 'NE PLUS ULTRA', 1824-36.

CAMBRIAN POTTERY MARKS

Transfer 'Mignionette', 1824-36.

Transfer 'CHINESE VIEWS', 1824-36.

Raised pad 'CYMRO STONE CHINA', 1836-50.

Impressed 'DILLWYN', 1824-50.

Impressed 'DILLWYN SWANSEA', 1824-50.

Impressed 'DILLWYN & Co' with numerals 1-8 or a cross or star, 1836-50.

Impressed 'DILLWYN SWANSEA' with number 3, 1836-50.

Transfer 'WHAMPOA IMPROVED STONE-WARE DILLWYN & Co', 1836-50.

Transfer 'LAZULI', 1836-50.

Transfer 'IMPROVED SAXON BLUE DILLWYN & Co', 1836-50.

Transfer 'OTTOMAN', 1836-50.

CAMBRIAN POTTERY MARKS

Transfer 'AMOY DILLWYN & Co',
1836-50.

Transfer 'CUBA
DILLWYN & Co', 1836-
50.

Transfer 'Oriental BASKET', 1836-50.

Transfer 'IMPROVED WILLOW D & Co',
1836-50.

Transfer 'Tea Leaf', 1836-50.

Transfer 'DILLWYN'S ETRUSCAN WARE', 1831-50.

Transfer 'Opaque China', 1831-50.

Transfer 'EVANS & GLASSON SWANSEA BEST
GOODS', 1850-62.

Transfer 'STONEWARE', 1850-62.

Impressed 'EVANS & GLASSON SWANSEA' with a
numeral, 1850-62.

Transfer 'D. J. EVANS & Co. FLORAL',
1862-70.

Transfer 'D. J. EVANS & Co. WOODBINE', 1862-70.

Transfer 'D. J. EVANS & Co. SWANSEA
VERANDAH', 1862-70.

Transfer 'D. J. EVANS & Co. SWANSEA', 1862-70.

Transfer 'D. J. EVANS & Co. SWANSEA BIRDS', 1862-70.

CAMBRIAN POTTERY MARKS

Early Glamorgan pottery is impressed 'BAKER BEVANS &
IRWIN' in a horseshoe over the Prince of Wales's feathers, and
'SWANSEA'. Later both the Prince of Wales's feathers and 'BAKER
BEVANS & IRWIN' appear alone. Transfer cartouches include
the initials 'B B & I', and 'G P Co/S' is found incorporated into
the design of early ship transfers. An S also appears as part of
Glamorgan willow pattern.

Impressed 'H', an early mark used by Baker Bevans & Irwin before 1820.

Impressed 'BAKER BEVANS & IRWIN SWANSEA', 1814-39.

Impressed 'BAKER BEVANS & IRWIN' with a numeral, 1814-39.

Baker Bevans & Irwin, impressed 1814-39.

Baker Bevans & Irwin, impressed 1814-39.

Baker Bevans & Irwin, impressed 1814-39.

Transfer 'Opaque China B B & I', 1814-39.

Transfer 'B B & I', 1814-39,

Transfer 'Opaque China B B & I', 1814-39.

Transfer 'COTTAGE GIRL B B & I', 1814-39.

Transfer 'Haymaker B B & I', 1814-39.

Transfer 'B. B. & I. Harper', 1814-39.

Transfer 'Vine B B & I', 1814-39.

Transfer 'GOTHIC BORDER B. B. & I.', 1814-39.

Transfer 'Campania B B & Co', 1814-39.

GLAMORGAN POTTERY MARKS

Ynysmeudwy pottery is impressed 'YNYSMEUDWY POTTERY', 'YNYSMEUDWY POTTERY SWANSEA VALE' or 'YMP', and transfer cartouches include the name 'WILLIAMS' or the initials 'WW'.

Impressed 'YMP', 1849-77.

YNYSMEUDWY POTTERY MARK

Transfer 'GEM WILLIAMS', 1849-60.

Transfer 'WILLIAMS IVY', 1849-60.

YNYSMEUDWY POTTERY MARKS

Impressed marks on early ware from Llanelly include 'SWP', 'SOUTH WALES POTTERY' and/or the name or initials of 'W. CHAMBERS JUN.', arranged in two circles or a horseshoe. 'S.W.P.' and 'SOUTH WALES POTTERY' are found in transfer cartouches. From 1855 to 1875 the impressed mark 'IRON-STONE CHINA' is found alone and with a registration mark on certain patterns. Transfer marks include the initials 'C & H' and 'W T H', which after 1877 were replaced by the initials 'G & D', sometimes with the initial 'L'. Later wares were marked 'LLANELLY', 'LLANELLY POTTERY' or 'LLANELLY ART POTTERY', stencilled or written in black or green.

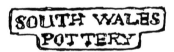

Impressed 'SOUTH WALES POTTERY', 1839-55.

Impressed 'SOUTH WALES POTTERY' with a numeral, 1839-55.

Transfer 'MILAN S.W.P.', 1839-55.

Transfer 'PANORAMA SOUTH WALES POTTERY', 1839-55.

44. *Ynysmeudwy jug, 318 mm high, and bowl, 368 mm in diameter. The jug is marked with a cartouche of the pattern name 'IVY' with 'Williams' below, and a transferrer's mark, a circle with a dot in the middle. The bowl has an additional impressed 'YMP'. Made between 1845 and 1860.*

Transfer 'DAMASK BORDER SOUTH WALES POTTERY', 1839-55.

Transfer 'BOMBAY JAPAN South Wales Pottery', 1839-55.

Impressed 'SOUTH WALES POTTERY
W. CHAMBERS', 1839-55.

Transfer 'ORIENTAL WC Jn LP',
1839-55.

C & H.

Transfer registration
mark for 'FLORA C & H',
1855-8.

Impressed 'IRONSTONE CHINA',
1855-75.

Transfer 'NAUTILUS C & H', 1855-8.

Transfer 'COLANDINE W.T.H.', 1858-75.

Transfer 'Asiatic Pheasants G & DL', 1877-1907.

Stencilled 'Llanelly', 1900-22.

Hand-written 'Llanelly', 1900-22.

SOUTH WALES POTTERY MARKS   33

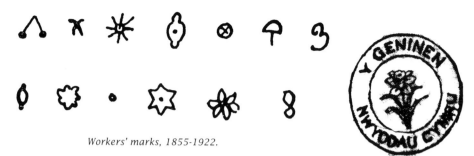

Workers' marks, 1855-1922.

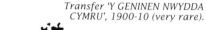

Transfer 'Y GENINEN NWYDDA CYMRU', 1900-10 (very rare).

Transfer 'LLANELLY POTTERY WALES', 1900-10 (very rare).

Transfer retailer's mark 'F. PRIMAVESI & SONS CARDIFF & SWANSEA'. This frequently appears on pottery made in South Wales.

SOUTH WALES POTTERY MARKS

45. South Wales Pottery ironstone plate, 270 mm in diameter, decorated with the 'Llanelly Bouquet' transfer pattern in blue, impressed 'IRONSTONE CHINA'. This pattern was registered during W. T. Holland's ownership of the factory and was also used on other items including meat plates and jugs.

46. South Wales Pottery ironstone tureen with strainer and lid, 280 mm high, decorated with the 'Flora' transfer pattern in blue-black, the lid and tureen impressed with 'W'. This pattern is sometimes encountered with a registration trademark and was the second registered by Holland. Also found in green, it is really a series of floral designs, which were shown at the 1861 Exhibition in London.

47. Glamorgan jug, 165 mm high, decorated with a purple transfer design commemorating the passing of the Reform Bill in 1832, marked 'B B & I Opaque China'. This distinctive shape was decorated in a variety of ways and was also extensively used at the South Wales Pottery, though apparently with a differently shaped handle.

Much South Wales pottery is unmarked and identification can be hazardous. The trademarks of retailers such as Primavesi appear not only on South Wales pieces but also on Staffordshire wares. Ready-made moulds, copper plates, etc, were available through Staffordshire trade suppliers. Factories freely copied one another, unhampered by copyright restrictions, even going so far as taking moulds directly off competitors' popular lines. These show up as exact copies, significantly smaller due to shrinkage during firing. The movement of workers, trading between factories and the appropriation of redundant plant and stock also complicate identification but in the absence of marks pieces can often be identified by a combination of other factors.

35

48. (Right) Distinctively shaped jug, mid nineteenth century, 178 mm high, decorated with a blue transfer and marked 'GEM' in a cartouche, with 'WILLIAMS' below. The shape is thought to be unique to the Ynysmeudwy factory and this marked piece enables the attribution of unmarked jugs of similar shape. (Left) Similar unmarked jug decorated in the 'Gaudy Welsh' manner. Copper lustre jugs of identical size and shape are found. 'Gaudy Welsh' and copper lustre items are found in vast quantities in Wales, and though most are presumed to have originated outside Wales this evidence suggests that some at least were locally produced. This is confirmed by sherds from the Ynysmeudwy factory site.

CERAMICS FOR USE AND DISPLAY

Ceramics have played an important part in Welsh social life and pottery was central to certain folk customs. The Ewenny wassail bowls described earlier were used in Glamorgan at New Year, and in Carmarthenshire wassail bowls and puzzle jugs were part of All Hallows' Eve celebrations. Young men throughout Wales gave fairings (ceramics purchased at fairs) as courting gifts. Pottery would have been an essential part of a woman's contribution to her marriage and would have been given at the gatherings or biddings held before weddings, when debts were paid and loans made to the young couple. Copper lustre jugs filled with jam were traditionally sold in markets in west Wales.

Utilitarian goods and cheap household china were always in constant demand, but the collection and display of decorative ceramics played an important role in defining status and identity in Welsh family life. This is exemplified by the personalised dedications, names and dates commemorating important family occasions found inscribed on all manner of

wares. The practice relied on personal contact which could be easily maintained only with a fairly local producer.

Welsh women often used the proceeds from the sale of eggs or butter to purchase pottery for use and, more significantly, display in the home. There is an early reference in the Hawarden Register of Births to a woman giving birth whilst travelling from Dolgellau to Buckley to buy pots. Large Delft-ware chargers were still being made in Liverpool in the late eighteenth century and sent to border fairs in Chester, where they were bought in large quantities, undoubtedly for display, by Welsh farmers from inaccessible mountain districts. Pottery was more usually bought from itinerant traders or potmen who hawked wares around isolated farms and villages and at fairs and markets.

Pride in the hearth was expressed through the contents of the home, which included specific items of furniture made from native Welsh oak and a ceramic display. The North Wales farmhouse would typically contain a grandfather clock, a dresser with a cupboard base, a cupboard with two or three sections (*cwpwrdd deuddarn* or *cwpwrdd tridarn*) and a glass-fronted cupboard (*cwpwrdd gwdyr*). The dresser would have been dressed with a blue and white dinner service, with 'Willow' or 'Asiatic Pheasants' the most popular patterns. Mugs, jugs and ornaments were generally displayed in the glass cupboard or hung from shelves and beams.

In South Wales the dresser normally had an open base for large pots and crocks used in the dairy. The top might have held a more colourful display. Llanelly 'Colandine' was popular for the dinner service, and in addition there might have been hand-painted plates such as the 'Persian Rose', Llanelly 'Cockerel' plates, sponge-decorated cawl bowls (cawl is a traditional lamb stew) and jugs in sets of three from large to small, suspended from hooks in the dresser shelves. With the dresser and clock there would have been a glazed corner cupboard (*cwpwrdd cornel*), containing tea services and ornaments of various kinds.

Transfer-decorated dinner services, Staffordshire figures, cow creamers, lustre jugs and 'Gaudy Welsh' pottery were popular throughout Wales. Only a proportion of the ceramics

50. *South Wales Pottery plate, 220 mm in diameter, decorated with the 'Colandine' transfer pattern in brown, marked with a pattern cartouche surrounded by bamboo sticks with 'W. T. H.' underneath, made between 1858 and 1875. This design is also found in blue, green, black and pink and, to judge by the quantities still found in Wales, was, with the 'Asiatic Pheasants', the most popular design the factory produced. It is used on whole dinner services and was frequently marked with the Primavesi retailer's mark. This design was previously thought to have been exclusive to the South Wales Pottery, but some pieces have been discovered with a Bovey Tracey mark, suggesting an intriguing link with the Devon factory.*

used and collected was supplied by Welsh potteries, but local needs and tastes defined a lucrative market to which local producers clearly responded. But by the beginning of the twentieth century imports from Germany offered stiff competition for the home market and many pottery workers became retailers. Llanelly supported three china shops and by 1900 a shop in nearby Ammanford received regular consignments of imported German china.

The Welsh public enjoyed pottery that signalled status and family pride yet brightened and enlivened their dark homes. This distinctive preference continued well into the twentieth century. A prominent feature of many Welsh homes today is a Welsh dresser, decorated in a traditional manner with pottery that has been handed down through the family and has treasured associations, or equally valued pieces collected in accordance with traditional tastes. Reminiscing in 1953 about her childhood in Llandefeilog in Carmarthenshire, Ethel Davies wrote: 'I shall always recall with pleasure the stone floors and the charm of the old dark polished oak furniture – the grandfather clock with its loud tick; a corner cupboard laden with china tea services and, above all, the beautiful oak dresser with its blue and white willow pattern dishes and plates.'

FURTHER READING

Hallesy, Helen L. *The Glamorgan Pottery.* Gomer, 1995.
Hughes, Gareth, and Pugh, Robert. *Llanelly Pottery.* Llanelli Borough Council, 1990.
Jenkins, Dilys. *Llanelly Pottery.* DEB, Swansea, 1968.
Lewis, J.M. *Medieval Pottery and Metal-ware in Wales.* National Museum of Wales, 1978.
Lewis, J.M. *The Ewenny Potteries.* National Museum of Wales, 1982.
Nance, E. Morton. *The Pottery and Porcelain of Swansea and Nantgarw.* B. T. Batsford, London, 1942.
Pryce, P.D., and Williams, S.H. 'Swansea Blue and White Pottery', *Antique Collecting,* volume 7, numbers 1, 2 and 3 (1972).
Pugh, Robert. *Welsh Pottery: The Potteries of South Wales.* Towy, Bath, 1995.
Tyler, Sheila. *Buckley Pottery* (exhibition catalogue). Mostyn Art Gallery, Llandudno, 1983.
Vincentelli, Moira. *Talking Pots.* University College of Wales, 1992.

PLACES TO VISIT

Before travelling, intending visitors are advised to telephone to find out the opening times and to establish that relevant items will be on display.

Buckley Library, Buckley, Flintshire CH7 2EF. Telephone: 01244 549210. A collection of Buckley pottery is on display.

Carmarthen Museum, Abergwili, Carmarthen SA31 2JG. Telephone: 01267 231691. Ceramics from the South Wales Pottery.

Ceramic Gallery, Arts Centre, University College of Wales, Penglais, Aberystwyth, Cardiganshire SY23 3DE. Telephone: 01970 622460.

Glynn Vivian Art Gallery, Alexandra Road, Swansea, Glamorgan SA1 5DZ. Telephone: 01792 655006 or 651738.

The Mansion House, Bryncaerau, Parc Howard, Llanelli, Carmarthenshire SA15 3LJ. Telephone: 01554 772029. A collection of pieces from the South Wales Pottery.

Museum of Welsh Life, St Fagans, Cardiff CF5 6XB. Telephone: 01222 569441. Ewenny Pottery is on view and the old kiln from the Ewenny Pottery has been reconstructed on site.

National Museum and Gallery Cardiff, Cathays Park, Cardiff CF1 3NP. Telephone: 01222 397951.

Swansea Museum, Victoria Road, Swansea, Glamorgan SA1 1SN. Telephone: 01792 653763.